To : _____

From : _____

Collins Publishers San Francisco

Souvenirs

gifts from the garden

Kathryn Kleinman & Michaele Thunen

First published 1994 by Collins Publishers San Francisco

Copyright © 1994 by Kathryn Kleinman and Michaele Thunen

Produced and Art Directed by Kathryn Kleinman and Michaele Thunen

Photography: Kathryn Kleinman

Styling: Michaele Thunen

Text: Ethel Brennan and Michaele Thunen

Design: Jennifer Barry

Illustration and Calligraphy: Lauren Allard

Library of Congress Cataloging-in-Publication Data

Kleinman, Kathryn.

Souvenirs: gifts from the garden / Kathryn Kleinman & Michaele Thunen.

p.   cm.

ISBN 0-00-255347-3

1. Flower arrangement—Pictorial works. 2. Flowers—Pictorial works. 3. Fruit—Pictorial works.
4. Vegetables—Pictorial works. 5. Table setting and decoration—Pictorial works. 6. Flower
arrangement. I. Thunen, Michaele. II. Title

SB449.K565 1994   93-49823

745.92—dc20   CIP

Printed in Italy by Arnaldo Mondadori LTD.   10 9 8 7 6 5 4 3 2 1

For all the Mothers in our lives

to my Mother Eloise, and to Rosie and Ellie
Thank you for all of your love and support--
your vision and inspiration.

All my love, Kathryn

to my Mother Betty Jane, Grammy, Pat,
Lida and Aunt Mary

Your love of flowers, the garden, and all
its special creatures introduced me to the
wonders of nature. I am forever grateful.

All my love, Michaele

Preface

We began this project in the rain of spring and collected all that nature had to offer. As we worked through the seasons, we entered gardens glistening with early morning dew or cast with the deepening shades of late afternoon light. Throughout the year, nature was our workshop, and our teachers were the passionate gardeners and naturalists who shared their enthusiasms and their knowledge, as well as their gardens with us. Most of all, creating this book affirmed for us the magical spirit of the garden and of nature, which brings tranquility and joy, even in the midst of work. As we worked to realize our vision of arrangements that reflect nature's harmony, we rediscovered the peace and wonder we first felt as children, when an upturned leaf revealed a ladybug, or an ice-covered plant set us to dreaming of crystal palaces and fairy tales. A seemingly chaotic collection of branches and flowers, when arranged by Michaele and brought to life by Kathryn in her photographs, reveals the microcosm of nature's order, as well as the surprise simplicity of the garden's mystery. The continual engagement, with each other, with plants and flowers, with light and water, and with all the wonderful people who played a part in the creation of this book, has enriched us both. The experiences, both fleeting and enduring, have touched us emotionally and intellectually, and we come away from this very special project with deeply etched memories that link us ever more firmly to the natural world we love.

Inspirations

Awakenings

Radiance

Promises

Tranquility

Notes

Inspirations

Souvenirs. A single garden peony in an old jelly jar.

An afternoon's bounty of wild berries in a porcelain

bowl, some still clinging to their twisting vines.

Nature's extraordinary gifts. Gathered in gardens,

SEASONS

orchards, meadows, and forests. Collections from

just outside the back door; walks through the woods,

IMPRESSIONS

or lazy afternoon drives through the country.

Souvenirs change with the seasons. A profusion

REMEMBRANCE

of blossoms arranged into a bouquet. Tangles of soft

grasses and spring wildflowers fill heirloom vases.

Bittersweet, rosehips, and empty birds' nests; the

dried remembrances of seasons gone by.

Peaceful moments. Baskets of rain-scented spring blossoms,

armloads of bright summer sunflowers, pockets full of fall's earthy

must-scented acorns. Magical souvenirs, some fragile

and fleeting, some eternal and everlasting. Ephemeral as a bouquet of

red poppies dropping petals at the slightest touch. Enduring as a

bowl of winter gourds and dried ears of corn, warming the kitchen table.

Nature changes from one season to the next. Reflecting the cycle of life:

birth, death, rebirth. The brilliance and radiance of spring and summer.

Energy. Vibrance. Gentle rains. Long days full of sunshine

and warmth. The subtleties of fall and winter. Tranquility. Solitude.

Falling leaves. The first snowfall. Late afternoon sunsets.

Life and nature, as certain as the sun and moon. Constant and forever.

Awakenings

Spring, a time of awakening. Everything is clear and fragrant. The perfume of cool white lilacs and sweet garden peonies scents the air. The dampness of early morning mist and surprise rain showers nurtures the earth. Dancing reflections of light fill the sky. Rainbows shimmer from the surfaces of streams flooded with icy waters, fresh from the melting snow. Tender new grass and bulb shoots emerge from the warming earth. Tree branches display veils of soft green buds, soon to unfold into delicate pink blossoms.

To see a hillside white with dogwood bloom is to know a particular ecstasy

of beauty, but to walk the gray Winter woods and find the buds which will resurrect

that beauty in another May is to partake of continuity.   —Hal Borland

*Treasures gathered from
the garden are necessarily in step
with nature's patterns.
Whatever comes indoors in the
bucket or basket will
harmonize with the season.
In spring, ranunculus
and budding branches, whether
amassed into a large, dramatic
arrangement or placed
simply in a water-filled mason jar,
complement one another
and immediately shout springtime.*

The arrival of spring opens
doors to the outside, away from the
cozy fireplaces of winter.
The gentle warmth of the sunshine
prompts picnics and al fresco
parties. Tables are laid with colorful
linens and decorated with fresh
bouquets of wildflowers. Morning
coffee and tea no longer
serve to fight the chilly air, but
become an excuse to sit
quietly for a moment and enjoy
the cool morning dew.

Live in each season as it passes: Breathe the air,

drink the drink, taste the fruit, and resign yourself to the

influences of each. —*Henry David Thoreau*

Sparse branches of flowering quince, their buds open, embedded in a
homemade ice bucket. Alone or mixed with other flowers, the effect is stunning;
a frosty bottle of vodka wrapped within an icy cylinder of crystallized water.

One of the daintiest
joys of spring is the falling
of soft rain among
blossoms. The shining and
apparently weightless
drops come pattering into
the maytree with
a sound of soft laughter;
one alights on a
white petal with a little
inaudible tap;

24

then petal and raindrop

fall together down the

steeps of green and white,

accompanied by troops of

other petals, each with

her attendant drop and her

passing breath of scent.

—Mary Webb

*Arrangements reflect the
natural structure of the garden.
The layers are created by trees,
shrubs, and low-growing perennials
and annuals. Here, the full
branches of the dogwood tree cap
the arrangement just as
the trees cap the garden setting.
Beneath the branches nestle
smaller-growing shrubs—lace cap
and snowball viburnum. At the base,
hellebore and nicotiana represent
the first level of the garden, those
plants closest to the earth.*

The secret to long-lived
cut flowers is water. As soon as they
come from the garden
or the florist, cut a bit off each stem
and plunge them into a full
bucket or basin. To best condition
them, leave them to stand
overnight in water before arranging.
When arranging, again clip
the ends of the stems to ensure the
easy absorption of fresh water.

The iris standing in the marsh: so blue,

Its roots have drunk the sky's reflected hue. —Ho-o

aster and the blossoming of apple trees coincide in some areas of the world. A branch of sweet-smelling apple blossoms in an earth-toned pot becomes a graceful framework for the pastels of dyed eggs. Thin ribbons threaded through the hollowed shells begin this fun and festive project for children.

"Yes, they are tiny growing things and they might be crocuses or snowdrops

or daffodils," she whispered. She bent very close to them and sniffed the fresh scent of

the damp earth. —Frances Hodgson Burnett, The Secret Garden

Nature's complements. Heavy lemons dipping from their branches into a patch of purple hyacinth, delicate iris perched atop upright stems. When brought together indoors, these contrasting elements harmonize in an evocative display of color and form. The flowers' soft, bearded crowns offset the robust fullness of the fruit.

Nothing that is can pause or stay;

The moon will wax, the moon will wane,

The mist and cloud will turn to rain

The rain to mist and cloud again,

Tomorrow be today.

—Henry Wadsworth Longfellow

A Chinese cabbage has porcelain-like leaves that fold and wrap, one clasping over another to form a tight cylinder. When immersed in a clear vase of water, the leaves become a luminous vessel perfect for holding a bouquet of lacy lavender hydrangea. Look at the garden with an unprejudiced eye, and a cabbage or a melon becomes a vase, a branch of almonds a companion to roses.

The dangling clusters
of pale purple flowers and
full greenery of wisteria
mask the inner beauty of its
twisting, gnarled branches.
Wisteria and clematis wind
through trellises and arbors,

creating densely woven
canopies of lush green foliage
and lightly-scented blooms,
which will soon drop hundreds
of tiny petals, carpeting
the ground below.

*A*s my Garden invites into it all the Birds of the Country, . . I value my garden more for it being full of Blackbirds than Cherries, and very frankly give them Fruit for their Songs.

—*Joseph Addison*

Scented herbs and flowers, such as lavender, sage, verbena, and tiny heliotrope,

have been used throughout time to sweeten the air. In the past, ladies carried small

nosegays known as Tussie Mussies through the streets of London to fend off

offensive odors. Dried lavender flowers, tied with snatches of ribbon into small sachets,

perfumed drawers of delicates and kept moths away from precious linens.

May Day is a forgotten holiday
that ushers in the spring. Anonymous
gifts of handmade baskets
filled with wildflowers and garlands
of scented lilac were once left
on doorsteps of friends and neighbors
to celebrate the season.
White wild iris, blossoming coriander,
dainty forget-me-nots,
and tiny blue muscari enveloped by
baskets woven of ivy leaves
and curling pink jasmine vines make
sweet-smelling spring gifts.

It always seems to me that the herbaceous peony is the very epitome of June. Larger than any rose, it has something of the cabbage rose's voluminous quality; and when it finally drops from the vase, it sheds its vast petticoats with a bump on the table, all in an intact heap, much as a rose will suddenly fall, making us look from our book or conversation, to notice for one moment the death of what had still appeared to be a living beauty.

— *Vita Sackville-West*

A garden full of peonies. Creamy white. Pale pink.

Vivid fuschia. The showy blooms owe their splendor to one of nature's marvels.

Each spring as the buds swell and begin to open, ants crawl between

the petals and deep into the hearts of the flowers, helping them to unfold.

Radiance

Summer, the season of vivid contrasts. Pale white heat. Explosions of color: Blue bachelor's buttons, purple, pink, and magenta dahlias celebrate the season. Warmth and radiance fuse. Golden wheat fields and seas of yellow sunflowers spread beneath bright blue skies. Fruit tree branches dangle close to the ground, heavy with fragrant ripe peaches, nectarines, and apricots. Seductively, summer inspires lazy moments beneath the cool shade of branching walnut trees.

The most familiar and
ordinary of flowers can become
the most special. There
is something precious about the
simplicity of grasses, daisies,
and dandelions, all too frequently
overlooked. Meandering
together they form an arrangement
that is extraordinary
in its quiet unpretentiousness.

When you can put your foot on seven daisies summer is come.

—Traditional Proverb

*T*he splendor of color attracts us in many ways. It can be as simple as a single white flower emerging from the shadows of a room, or as dramatic as the vivid contrasts found in complementary colors.

Transparent, paper-thin poppy petals in silky shades of coral, orange, and red are propped atop long,

delicately twisting stems. They create a burst of color against the pale green backdrop of spring wheat fields and

meadow grasses, and are sprinkled through nature like left-over confetti from a child's garden party.

Their vibrant color will soon fade and the petals will drop away, leaving crowns of star-shaped seed pods.

Still, in a way, nobody sees a flower, really.

It is so small. We haven't the time and to see takes time,

like to have friends takes time. —Georgia O'Keeffe

Summer has two palettes. The first is vibrant and full of saturated colors. Striped beach umbrellas, glowing ripe fruits, high mountain lakes, and the shocking golds and reds of nasturtiums and zinnias in the garden. The second is subdued and pastel. Fresh peach ice cream, clear summer skies reflected in shaded streams, and the muted hues of lavender hydrangea and soft pink penstemon.

One of the greatest pleasures of life is the mystery of nature.

Every flower, branch or fruit gathered and arranged brings

a hint, a remembrance, of that mystery indoors.

The simple combination of well-beaten egg whites, very fine sugar, and
the colorful petals of unsprayed roses produces crystallized candies. These sweetly perfumed,
glass-like treats smell and taste of rosewater and summer gardens.

*I was walking alone in my garden;
there was great stillness among the
branches and flowers, and more than common
sweetness in the air; I heard a low and
pleasant sound, and I knew not whence it
came. At last I saw the broad leaf of a
flower move, and underneath I saw a green
procession of creatures, of the size and
colour of green and grey grasshoppers, bearing
a body laid out on a rose-leaf, which
they buried with songs, and then disappeared.
It was a fairy funeral.* —William Blake

A delicate bouquet of early summer roses—Dainty Maid, Antigua,

and Gold Medal—along with soft green apricots still on their branches, brings the fragrances,

colors, and warmth of the season to a quiet corner of the home.

Berries are nature's sweet treasures, protected by their prickly vines or nestled away beneath the shade of their leaves. Wild brambles overflowing along roadsides are irresistible. Long hours are spent cautiously picking berries, and for every one that goes into the bucket, two become a sweet reward. Precariously struggling with the prickly vines and reaching for the plumpest, juiciest gems, thoughts of sweet-smelling homemade jams and pies overcome scratched and purple-stained fingers.

Bright yellow sunflower heads interlace with
the thornless brambles of green rosehips to form a
summer wreath. This whimsical gift lasts throughout
the year, changing with the seasons as the
sunflowers gradually fade to brown.

Tiny yellow pear tomatoes and spidery mustard-colored coreopsis grow together in the kitchen garden, entangling their vines and intermingling their fruits and blooms. These gardens are woven from a palette of seasonal vegetables, fruits, and flowers, bursting with a treasure trove of hidden wonders.

. . . the beautiful bearded iris—
the clear blue of Symphony and the
tantalizing golden brown
tinged with wine pink of Cinnamon
Toast. The Flowers go on and
on flowering everyday. One dies and
another opens and they flower
for a full four weeks. There are many
other colours, purple, pure gold,
dull reds with light brown frilly
translucent petals. They give
and give and only ask for the sun to
bake their roots so they can
make their flowers for next year.
—Joan Wolfenden

A delight to eat, the artichoke is the bud of a thistle, and is as striking

in arrangements as on a luncheon plate. As the buds mature and grow larger,

the leaves open to form a crown around a brilliant purple flower.

It is the simple things of life that make living worthwhile,

the sweet fundamental things such as love and duty, work and

rest and living close to nature. —*Laura Ingalls Wilder*

Nasturtiums, with their curling vines, edible flat leaves, and peppery orange and yellow flowers, reach wildly in all directions, cloaking their surroundings. Apple trees are often encircled by densely woven carpets of nasturtiums, whose pungent aroma wards off the attacks of woolly aphis.

Promises

Fall, the season of rich abundance and hushed

anticipation. Overflowing baskets of apples,

quince, and persimmons. Hidden clusters of

FALL

narcissus, daffodil, and tulip bulbs, tucked deep

beneath the ground. Waiting. The promise of

ABUNDANCE

tiny seeds lying under a carpet of dried grasses.

A time of urgency and restlessness. The rustling

ANTICIPATION

whispers of windblown leaves signal the change

in light. Autumn is aglow. Collections of

pumpkins, acorns, and seed pods form a radiant

palette of gold, amber, and burgundy.

As days cool, sunlight fades, and colors turn, nature's late offerings ripen on

vines and trees. Sticky sweet persimmons and figs join speckled pears and piles of juicy grapes to

bring the bounty indoors. Their colors complement the muted yellows and oranges of loosely bunched

garden roses, whose hips are beginning to replace the full, fragrant blooms.

The summer
still hangs
heavy and sweet
with sunlight
as it did last year.
The autumn
still comes
showering gold and crimson
as it did last year.

The winter
still sings
clean and cold and white
as it did last year.
The spring still comes
like a whisper in the dark night.
It is only I who have changed.
—Charlotte Zolotow, "Change"

*In the fall, heavy clusters of purple grapes hang beneath a canopy of
glowing leaves whose color changes first to yellow, then deepens to shades of red and
crimson. The hidden fruit becomes a treasure trove for migrating birds.*

Working in the garden . . . gives me a profound feeling of inner peace. Nothing here is in a hurry. There is no rush toward accomplishment, no blowing of trumpets. Here is the great mystery of life and growth. Everything is changing, growing, aiming at something, but silently, unboastfully, taking its time.

—*Ruth Stout*

The simplest displays of nature's gifts can be the most pleasing. A collection of flowers

placed casually in a creamware pitcher, a mason jar, or an old milk bottle becomes a showpiece. A freestanding

collection of fruits, vegetables, and blooming bulbs becomes a dramatic still life.

Bulbs hold life inside, just waiting to burst into bloom. Forcing narcissus and amaryllis in

containers brings the excitement of new growth indoors. From the green stalks' first peek at daylight,

the anticipation of glorious blossoms enlivens the home. Gifts of bulbs pass the pleasure on to others.

A small box, covered with a brocade-like wrapping of fall leaves, makes an enduring souvenir.

Even if something is left undone, everyone must take time to sit still and watch the leaves turn.

—Elizabeth Lawrence

Pumpkins and squashes in myriad shapes, sizes, and colors become a fall staple. The pulp can be made into soups and pies, the shells carved into jack-o'-lanterns or containers for flowers. A grouping along entryway steps surrounded by the wiry branches of bittersweet vines adds a burst of color and festivity.

The brilliant orange of persimmons enlivens bouquets. Gently packed into an excelsior-lined wooden crate, then bound with a wide taffeta ribbon, the fruits become a colorful and bountiful gift. The Fuyu variety is ready to eat when crisp like an apple. The Hachiya variety must first soften, then the sweet, juicy pulp is ready for baking into cookies, cakes, and puddings.

*P*ersimmon trees signal the changing seasons. The golden green leaves have curled and dropped to the ground, leaving bare branches in anticipation of winter's coming landscape. The fruits, still hard and caramel colored, will continue to ripen into the first frosts.

Fall is a time for the warmth of fireside evenings with friends. Brandy infused with the sweet flavor of ripe pears makes a special gift to share. Tie a clear bottle to a branch of a Bartlett pear tree just as the tree has finished blooming and the fruit has begun to form. The secret is to cut the branch off the tree before the pear has grown large enough to touch the sides of the bottle.

My studio is full of fallen leaves. I cut them in their freshness and very soon they have floated down to the floor, faded, crisped up and quietly died. —Joan Wolfenden

*T*rees come out of acorns, no matter

how unlikely that seems. An acorn

is just a tree's way back into the ground.

For another try. Another trip through.

One life for another.

—*Shirley Ann Grau*

117

Sunflowers continue to unfold their showy blooms into late fall.

Their seeds hold promises of next year's splendor. A boxful, nestled in a

loosely woven basket and tied with bright, yellow-ruler ribbon,

is a gift from nature. A handful tossed back into the garden may thrive

and grow, or may become welcome morsels for hungry birds.

*Rosehips, the seed pods left behind by summer's roses, are as
varied in shape, size, and color as the heavily petaled blooms that
came before. The round, urn-shaped, or pointed hips, with their angled
brambles and brilliant colors, repeat the tapestry of nature.*

Autumn is a time of harvest and preparation. Seeds of flowers, vegetables, and grasses are collected and cleaned, then stored away for safekeeping until planting time. Each seed, no matter how tiny, holds within it the promise of life's unending cycle—nature's greatest gift.

Tranquility

Winter, the season of quiet reflection. Serenity and tranquility. A blanket of silver white snow covers nature's landscape. Inside. Warm and protected. Outside. Crisp and clear. Bare branches cast beautifully sculpted silhouettes. Fragrances of pine and woodsmoke linger. On warm kitchen windows, icy patterns come and go. Jack Frost. Flickering light from fireplaces and candles illuminates garlands of greens, baskets of oranges and lemons. Snowflakes fall silently.

Winter's soft palette paints
a serene landscape. Trees, now bare
of leaves, display their winter
coats of sculpted bark and pale green
moss. The green of ivy, the silver
gray of lamb's ears, and
the pure white of cyclamen blend
subtly in this silent season.

I prefer winter and fall, when you feel the bone structure in

the landscape—The loneliness of it—the dead feeling of winter. Something

waits beneath it—the whole story doesn't show. —Andrew Wyeth

Deep red hues and fragrant greens accentuate the spirit of the holiday season, a time of giving and sharing. Abandoned bird nests can be collected and filled with gilded acorns or foil-wrapped chocolates. Pine cones, stuffed with a mixture of suet and seeds, become a gift of appreciation to the hungry birds.

The snow, in bitter cold,

Fell all the night;

And we awoke to see

The garden white.

And still the silvery flakes

Go whirling by,

White feathers fluttering

From a grey sky.

Beyond the gate, soft feet

In silence go,

Beyond the frosted pane

White shines the snow.

—F. Ann Elliott, "The Snow"

Winter's harvests inspire a rich array of souvenirs. The drama of
bare, spindly alder branches mixed with the thick green stems and giant blooms
of amaryllis. The simplicity of mistletoe tucked into a favorite teapot along with
rosehips and paper whites. The warm welcome of a holiday wreath.

A crystalline bucket made of ice becomes a festive centerpiece for holiday entertaining. Adorned with scarlet berries, green foliage, or winter white flowers frozen into the ice, it keeps the bottle chilled and ready to share with friends.

*It is quite wonderful
how much colour is still to
be found and I find
some of my most successful
arrangements come
from these twigs and
berries, golden evergreen
bushes and bare
branches and fruits.*
— *Joan Wolfenden*

Flowers leave some of their fragrance in the hand that bestows them.
—*Chinese Proverb*

*Fruits, berries, and greenery collected in autumn can be made to
last throughout the winter. When temperatures fall outdoors, they are always
at hand to use in mantelpiece   still lifes, to bring color
to a reflective setting or to   combine with florist roses.*

The sculptural shapes of wiry brambles or bent twigs are gifts in their most natural state. The golden

hue of a crystallized branch is echoed in delicately gold-leafed acorns. By leaving room for the unexpected and allowing

for the element of surprise, the imagination can weave the commonplace into something new.

Few settings are more welcoming than collections of white flowers and

winter greenery bathed in the glow of flickering candlelight. Plates of homemade cookies, a bottle of Nocino,

and chestnuts ready for roasting complete a tableau of winter's inner warmth.

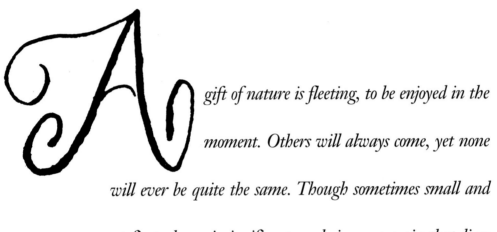 gift of nature is fleeting, to be enjoyed in the

moment. Others will always come, yet none

will ever be quite the same. Though sometimes small and

at first glance insignificant, each is a souvenir that lives

on in remembrances.

Notes

Gathering gifts from the garden brings excitement, the anticipation of creations to come. Choosing the right container, arranging the elements, then finding the perfect setting adds to the pleasure. Keeping a well-stocked floral pantry will ease the process. Knowing how to best condition the plant materials will prolong the enjoyment. Mastering techniques for securing the harvest in arrangements will allow for spontaneity.

Notes

Tools of the Floral Pantry

A variety of vases and containers for holding arrangements. Baskets, pitchers, heirloom vases, even old milk bottles and canning jars.

Sharp clippers, snips, scissors, and loppers for cutting materials.

A basket for gathering.

Buckets for holding water, vitamin B1, household bleach or floral preservative, and alum for conditioning.

A variety of marbles, rocks, floral foam, frogs, chicken wire, heavy plastic, and floral clay for securing stems.

Sphagnum moss and dried materials such as lichen, leaves, and acorns.

Toothpicks, skewers, floral picks, and floral tubes for adding fruits and vegetables to creations.

Wire of various gauges and floral tape for wreath making.

Wood glue, hot glue gun, and spray adhesive for adhering.

Gold-leafing supplies, including sizing, and gold and silver floral spray for holiday decorating.

A spray mister for adding moisture to indoor arrangements.

A watering can or pitcher for watering completed bouquets.

All of these materials are available through one or more of the following sources: floral shop, hardware store, garden center, hobby shop, art supply store, or garden catalogs.

Conditioning the Cuttings

Conditioning means to prepare the gatherings for arranging so that they will last as long as possible. It is best to cut plant materials either in the morning or in the evening, when the stems contain the most water. Cut the stem or branch on an angle just above a leaf node and immediately place it in a full bucket of water, to which vitamin B has been added. A couple of tablespoons per bucket will be sufficient. It is best to let the cuttings absorb water for at least twelve hours before arranging them.

Woody-stemmed cuttings, from trees, shrubs, and some vines, need additional conditioning. They have a harder time absorbing water, so the bottom of their stems must be crushed or split about three inches up. Fibrous-stemmed cuttings, such as daisies and chrysanthemums, also need this treatment. Remove leaves from branches and stems below the waterline in order to keep bacteria from growing, which shortens the life of the arrangement. Roses need to have their thorns cut off, not stripped, and their leaves removed, and will last longer if the ends are cut while underwater. Flowers and vines that have a milky sap, such as euphorbia and poppies, are best conditioned by singeing their ends, or placing the bottom two inches of the stems in boiling water for two to three minutes. Then they can be put in the conditioning bucket like all other flowers. Hydrangea lasts longer if its stems are placed in boiling water and then dipped in alum. Ivy and ferns like their leaves to stay moist, so they must stay fully immersed in water until just before arranging.

Allowing the plant materials to sit in a cool place while being conditioned is also beneficial. To revive flowers that have wilted, try recutting them, removing most leaves, then placing the entire stem, up to the neck, in water. This will often bring them back. For woody-stemmed branches that have wilted, dipping the stems in boiling water for one to two minutes and then putting them back into the conditioning bucket can be successful.

Securing the Gatherings

Securing flowers in a container can be done in a number of ways. First, prepare the container, by scrubbing it and filling it with tepid water. Add a few drops of household bleach to help prolong the life of the arrangement. The simplest way to secure flowers is to let the container itself hold them in place. Alternatively, use marbles, rocks, and even cut branches to provide a secure base from which to begin. If using oasis, or floral foam, make sure it has had plenty of time to completely absorb all the water that it can. If using a basket, line it with heavy plastic, then cut the oasis, pack it in tightly, and add water to the top. If a frog is your choice, use floral clay to adhere it to the bottom of the container, so it will stay securely in place. Chicken wire can be cut to fit over the mouth of a vase to create a grid to hold stems and branches in place. To begin arranging, make a fresh cut on each stem, except those that were singed or dipped in hot water. When the arrangement is completed, add as much bleach-infused water as needed, and replenish each day. If arranging in a vase, every second or third day remove the arrangement, holding it together, and rinse the bottoms of the stems under the faucet. Then add fresh water to the vase with a little bleach, and replace the bouquet. Setting the arrangement overnight in a cool spot, such as a garage or a porch, away from the dry heat of the house, will help prolong the life of your bouquet.

Awakenings

page 2: Ellen's Bouquet: *Pear blossoms, lily-flowering tulips, Angelique tulips, oxalis, and ivy*

page 6: *Pear blossoms, lily-flowering tulips, and Angelique tulips*

pages 10–11: Helie's Early Garden: *California poppies, forget-me-nots, sweet alyssum, delphinium, erysimum, euphorbia, stock, primrose, and ranunculus*

pages 12–13: Garden Roses and Figs: *Fisherman's Friend and Lady Elgin English roses, Ballerina spray rose, and figs on branches*

page 14: *Left*, Mixed Tulip Bouquet: *A variety of tulips, including Queen of the Night*

pages 14–15: *Right*, Helie's Tulip Garden: *Tulips, apple tree, birch trees, forget-me-nots, oxalis, and erysimum*

pages 16–17: *Pink and purple saucer magnolias and star magnolia*

page 18: *Top left*, Red Dogwood Arrangement: *Red dogwood, columbine, English Miss English roses, and artichokes on table. Top right, Red dogwood branch. Bottom right, Magnolia petals on a bed of grape hyacinth. Bottom left, Pink saucer magnolia branch*

page 19: Crabapple Bouquet: *Crabapple blossoms and ranunculus on a path lined with navel wort*

page 20: Quince Blossom Bouquet: *Blossoms and buds of quince shrub, bleeding heart, and ranunculus; with sweet pea on table*

page 21: *Top, Sink filled with crabapple blossoms, ranunculus, and allium. Bottom, Casablanca tulips, baby leeks, and spring radishes*

page 22: White Spring Blossom Bouquet: *Saucer magnolias, azaleas, dianthus, ranunculus, spirea, and allium*

page 23: *Left*, Vodka in Ice. Recipe: *Though the round freezing form used to create this photo is not readily available, a similar effect can be achieved by using a square-bottomed milk carton. Cut off the top of the empty carton and set a bottle of vodka in the bottom portion. Place flowering branches in the space between the bottle and the carton. (Flowers, leaves, berries, ribbons, sliced fruit, pinecones, and greenery are other possibilities. The simplest and most graphic arrangement is the most successful, as it lets light come through.) Fill the carton with distilled water almost to the top. Freeze. Check in one hour and push the branches down if they have worked their way upward. Continue to freeze for at least twenty-four hours. Remove from the freezer, tear off the milk carton, and serve on a silver tray. Top right, Saucer magnolia branch. Bottom right, Flowering crabapple branches* page 24: Top, Ranunculus and allium. Bottom, Dogwood, Japanese snow-ball viburnum, lace cap viburnum, and Francine Austin climbing rose

page 25: Top, Double Lilac Bouquet: Double lilacs. Bottom, Lace cap viburnum

pages 26–27: Essence of Spring Bouquet: Dogwood, Japanese snowball viburnum, lace cap viburnum, philadelphus, hellebore, nicotiana, veronica, and Francine Austin climbing rose

page 28: Pale pink tulips

page 29: Left, Lavender bearded iris

page 31: Egg Tree. Recipe: Soak a block of floral foam in water and fit tightly into a container. Cut any flowering or bare branch and secure it in the foam. Cover the foam with moss. Using ribbons, hang colored eggs, the shells emptied of their contents and dyed, on the branch. Blossoming Gravenstein apple tree branch

page 32: Spring Bulb Arrangement: Daffodils, hyacinth, tulips, scilla, grape hyacinth, ranunculus, and pansies

page 33: Left, Stone footpath bordered by tulips, anemones, rhododendron, grape hyacinth, pansies, alyssum, Dutch iris, and erysimum. Top right, Daffodils, California poppies, and anemones. Bottom right, Pansies

pages 34–35: Old apple tree with oxalis and delphinium

page 36: Top, Meyer lemon tree with grape hyacinth. Bottom, Bearded iris

page 37: Lemon and Iris Arrangement: Meyer lemon branches and bearded iris

pages 38–39: Iris in Zinc: Pacific Coast iris

page 40: Cabbage Bouquet: Napa cabbage and hydrangea

pages 42–43: Wisteria and oak trees

page 44: Top, Montana rubens clematis, white clematis, and wisteria. Bottom, Montana ruben clematis

page 45: Top, Wisteria. Bottom, Old wisteria vine

pages 46–47: Cherry Still Life: Bing cherries, chocolate cosmos, and philadelphus branch; on table are artichoke, bok choy, asparagus, and Chinese dogwood blossoms, backed by a wall of Boston ivy

page 48: Left, Lavender Sachet. Recipe: Collect an heirloom linen cloth and place a handful of dried lavender in the center. Secure with a beautiful ribbon tied around a stem of fresh lavender. Right, Ivy Leaf May Basket. Recipe: Find a large, shiny ivy leaf and shape it into a cone, securing with glue or a staple. Tie the ends of pink jasmine vine to the cone to make a handle, then fill basket with tiny flowers. Ivy leaf, jasmine vine, pink jasmine blossoms, forget-me-not, moliastrium, scarlet pimpernel, vinca minor, and allium are used here.

page 49: Tussie Mussie. Recipe: To make a small nosegay, start with a bunch of filler material such as leaves and vines. Poke flower stems into the bunch, working carefully so as not to damage the fragile stems. Then add more of the greenery to the outside and wire the stems together tightly at the base of the foilage. Tie a ribbon over the wire. Purple sage, green sage, salvia discolor, pale heliotrope, verbena rigida, sea lavender, and latifolium are used in this bouquet.

pages 50–51: Left, Paper May Basket. Recipe: Shape a piece of pastel construction paper into a cone and secure it with glue or a staple. Staple on a paper handle, then fill the basket with small spring flowers. Allium, blossoming coriander, grape hyacinth, forget-me-not, and lilac fill these May baskets.

page 51: Bottom, May basket with grape hyacinth, forget-me-not, and lily of the valley

pages 52–53: Pink peonies

page 54: Fuchsia peony

page 55: Top left, Sarah Bernhardt peony, larkspur, foxglove, and snap-dragon in garden. Top right, Peony bud with ants. Bottom right, Peonies. Bottom left, Peony and Apple Bouquet: A variety of peonies and newly formed apples on the branch

Radiance

pages 56–57: A field of sunflowers

page 58: Single Feverfew in a Glass: A bunch of single feverfew

page 59: Left, Adirondack Daisy Arrangement: Silver leaf daisy chrysanthemum, aster pillosus, and two varieties of sedge, including bronze, carex testaceaur and carex buchananii. Top right, A patch of common daisies. Bottom right, Single feverfew

page 60: Duchess of Edinburgh clematis blossom, oranges, and kumquats

page 61: Bottom, Orange tomatoes and fuchsia dahlia

page 62: A field of Icelandic poppies

page 63: Left, Icelandic poppy heads on galax leaves. Top right, Icelandic poppy. Bottom right, Flanders Field poppies

page 64: Icelandic poppy buds on Icelandic poppy leaves

page 65: Icelandic poppy head on galax leaves

pages 66–67: Summer's Pale Bouquet: Lace cap hydrangea, Queen Anne's lace, Iceberg spray rose, penstemon, scabiosa, salvia uliginosa, and butterfly bush

page 68: Cecile Brünner rose on baby dress

page 69: Left, Rose and Berry Bouquet: Belle Story English rose and blackberry blossoms. Top right, Francine Austin English rose. Bottom right, Penelope garden rose in sink

page 70: Garden Rose and Fig Arrangement: Figs on the branch, Fisherman's Friend and Lady Elgin English roses, and Ballerina spray rose

page 71: Candied Rose Petal. Recipe: Whisk two egg whites until foamy and paint onto unsprayed red or pink rose petals. Dip petals in superfine sugar and let dry on cookie sheet lined with waxed paper. Nestle into a special container and tie with a colorful bow.

pages 72–73: Helie's Shed: Climbing Royal Sunset and Talisman rambling roses, California poppies, forget-me-nots, and valerian

page 74: Rose and Apricot Arrangement: Tilton apricots on branch and Gold Medal, Dainty Maid, Antigua, and Cymbaline English roses

page 75: Left, Roses in Mercury Vase: Green apricots on the branch, dahlias, and Antigua and Helmut Schmidt English roses. Top right, Tournament of Roses and Just Joey garden roses, espaliered apple tree, and delphinium. Bottom right, Playboy garden rose

pages 76–77: Watermelon Still Life: Yellow watermelon, red watermelon, red seedless watermelon, musk melon, and mandevilla splendens vine in floral tubes with water

page 79: Berries, Berries, Berries: Strawberries, red raspberries, golden raspberries, blackberries, blueberries, currants, and boysenberries

page 80: Sunflowers on Blue Chair

page 81: Top, A field of sunflowers. Left, Green rosehips and Sun Gold sunflowers. Bottom right and left, Green Rosehip and Flower Wreath. Recipe: Shape three thornless rose brambles into a circular or heart-shaped wreath and wire the brambles together. Add flowers as desired. The flowers can be placed in floral tubes to keep them fresh.

With the flowers used here, the wreaths can also be allowed to dry. Right, Green rosehips, hydrangeas, sunflowers, and Queen Anne's lace

pages 82–83: Kitchen Garden Bouquet: *Coreopsis, sneeze weed, gaillardia, and yellow pear tomatoes on the vine*

page 83: Bottom, *Gaillardia*

page 84: Provence Bouquet: *Chocolate bearded iris, purple Sicilian artichokes, green almonds on the branch, blossoming olive branches, and wild oats*

page 85: Left, *Chocolate bearded iris.* Top right, *Green almonds on the branch and chocolate bearded iris.* Bottom right, *Sicilian artichokes and leaves in a wooden bowl*

page 86: Dahlia and Berry Bouquet: *Dahlias, raspberries on the vine, and golden raspberries*

page 87: Top left, *Miniature ball dahlia, Victor D, and semicactus dahlia, Roilyn.* Right, *Semicactus dahlia, Golden Years.* Bottom left, *Straight cactus dahlia, Jessica*

page 89: Nasturtium Bouquet

Promises

pages 90–91: *A road lined with liquidamber trees*

page 92: Autumn Rose Bouquet: *Abelia, rosehips, Annie Harkness, Lady Elgin, and Elegance English roses and below, grapes, pears, figs, persimmon, pomegranate, apple, and cherries*

page 93: Top, *Ripe grapes on the vine.* Bottom, *Virginia creeper on a wall*

page 94: Top, *Quince on the branch, Japanese maple, amaranth, spider chrysanthemums, wild anise, and rosehips.* Bottom, Fall Grass Arrangement: *Green rosehips, cattails, Johnson grass, northern sea oats, and triticale with a variety of melons and plums on the table*

page 95: Top, Quince and Chrysanthemum Bouquet: *Quince on the branch, alder branches with catkins, Japanese maple, spider chrysanthemums, amaranth, rosehips, and wild anise.* Bottom, *Kelsey plums, Santa Rosa plums, white wine grapes, and grape leaves in a wire basket*

page 96: Rose and Grape Bouquet: *Chablis and Sheer Bliss garden roses, sweet pea, and white wine grapes*

page 97: *A vineyard in autumn*

pages 98–99: Blue Pumpkins in Window: *Queensland Blue pumpkins, Blue Ballet Hubbard squash, and fresh Nokimis gourds*

page 100: *Queensland Blue pumpkin, Blue Indian corn, dried hydrangea, and Nokimis gourd*

page 101: Left, Maple Leaves and Roses: *Swan double garden rose and silver maple leaves.* Top right, *Autumn crocus.* Bottom right, White Pumpkins on Table: *Lumina pumpkins, Blue Ballet Hubbard squash, Delicata squash, feather corn, and amaryllis blossoms*

page 102: Left, *A variety of bulbs including anemone, ranunculus, tulip, crocus, fritillaria, allium, lily, species tulip, and narcissus.* Top right, Brocade Box. *Recipe: Collect a handful of fall-colored leaves—it is best to use all of the same variety—and a lidded cardboard box. Using spray adhesive on the backs of the leaves, affix them one at a time to the box. Completely cover the outside of the box bottom, and both the inside and the outside of the lid, overlapping leaves as needed.* Bottom right, *Pistacia leaves lining a box with paper white narcissis and tulip bulbs*

page 103: Fall Leaves in Waxed Paper. *Recipe: Collect brightly colored leaves and arrange them between two sheets of waxed paper. With a warm (not hot) iron, press the sheets together until the wax melts and binds the sheets to each other. Hang in a window to let the light come through.*

page 105: *Rouge Vis D'Etamps pumpkins, turban squash, Blue Ballet Hubbard squash, Golden Nugget squash, bittersweet vine, persimmon leaves, and potted evergreen candytuft*

page 106: Olive and Persimmon Arrangement: *Olives and Fuyu persimmons on the branch*

page 107: Top, Persimmon Line-up: *Tamopan, Hachiya, Fuyu, and Shomo persimmons with red rosehips.* Bottom, *Shomo persimmons in a crate of excelsior*

pages 108–109: *Hachiya persimmon tree*

page 110: *A variety of pears and fall leaves*

page 111: Pear Brandy. *Recipe: Just after a Bartlett pear tree has finished blooming, tie a bottle onto a branch and watch the pear grow inside. Before the fruit touches the sides of the bottle, cut the branch off, leaving as little stem on the pear as possible. Over medium heat, dissolve one-half cup of sugar in enough Mexican brandy to make two cups. Fill the bottle with the liquid. Cork and tie a ribbon around the neck.*

page 112: *Elm leaves in shed window*

page 113: Fall Hand-Tied Bouquet: *Japanese maple leaves and deadly nightshade branches tied with an agapanthus leaf*

page 114: Bottom, *Valley Oak acorn and leaf*

pages 114–115: Picture Frame. *Recipe: Buy inexpensive wooden picture frames and glue on dried materials to cover. Lichen, leaves, acorns, oak galls, moss, or sticks are all possibilities. It is best to keep it simple, using no more than one or two items per frame. Lichen, maul oak acorns and leaves, and Charles Austin English rose are shown here.*

page 116: Top, *A variety of acorns, from the California live oak, maul oak, valley oak, encina oak, and red oak, on a bed of magnolia leaves.* Bottom, *A bowl of acorns from various oak trees*

page 117: Top, *Dried American native persimmons with red oak acorns and oak leaves.* Bottom, *Pawpaw persimmons with red oak acorns and oak leaves*

page 118: Top, Sunflower Seed Box. *Recipe: Choose a special box and fill with unshelled sunflower seeds. Tie a small, fresh sunflower to the top using a bright, cheerful ribbon.* Bottom, *Liquidamber tree branches*

page 119: Fall Sunflower Bouquet: *Burgundy and rust sunflowers, Queen Anne's lace, Jewel of Oppar, and wild grasses; Asian pears and figs on the table; Boston ivy on the wall*

pages 120–121: Squash Line-up on Bench: *Heart of Gold squash, Blue Ballet Hubbard squash, Nokimis gourd, Crown of Thorns gourd, Golden Nugget squash, and Seckel, Bosc, red Bartlett, and Asian pears*

page 122: Rosehip Arrangement: *A variety of rosehips and persimmons*

page 123: Top, *Tamopan, Fuyu, and Shomo persimmons with rosehips.* Bottom, *Mountain ash trees with berries*

page 124: Top left, *A variety of seeds.* Top right, *Dried sunflower heads.* Bottom right, *Dried agapanthus heads.* Bottom left, *Dried rudbeckia*

pages 126–127: *Dried sunflower and wild fennel heads*

Tranquility

pages 128–129: *Evergreen trees covered with snow*

page 130: Winter Nosegay: *Dusty miller, santolina, English ivies, cyclamen, and lily of the valley*

page 131: Top, *Evergreen shrubs and pines covered with snow.* Bottom, *Gardenia shrubs under cloches, also called bell jars, which protect delicate plants and flowers from the frost*

page 132: Top left, *Bird's nest in evergreen tree.* Top right, Gold Leaf-Covered Box. *Recipe: Spray both sides of fresh galax or ivy leaves gold. Using spray adhesive on the backs of the leaves, affix them one at a time to a lidded cardboard box. Completely cover the outside of the box bottom, and both the inside and the outside of the lid. Fill the box with something special, then tie with a bright red or green ribbon.* Bottom right, Pinecone Bird Feeder. *Recipe: Melt beef suet and mix in chunky peanut butter, sunflower seeds, wild birdseed, thistle seed, and ground peanuts. Let the mixture cool, then stuff it into the cone. Hang the cone, along with dried corn cobs and sunflower heads, to feed the birds in winter.* Bottom left, *Poinsettia and rosehips*

page 133: Rosehip wreath shaped as a heart

page 134: Cedar garland with holly and poinsettias

page 135: Ilex Berry and Bird Nest: *Ilex berries and gardenia blossom*

page 136: Left, Mistletoe berry wreath. Top right, Amaryllis, nandina, and alder branches. Bottom right, Mistletoe, paper white narcissus, rosehips, and ornamental strawberry vine

page 137: Winter Branch Bouquet: *Alder branches, nandina leaves and berries, and amaryllis with red apples on table*

page 138: Bottom, Ilex berries

pages 138–139: Ice Bucket. *Recipe: Use an eight- to ten-gallon galvanized bucket and a two-liter plastic soda bottle for a mold. Cut the top off the soda bottle and fill the bottom with rocks or marbles. Set it in the center of the bucket. Place adornments—berries, flowers, ribbon, greenery, or whatever is in season—between the sides of the bucket and the soda bottle. Fill this area with distilled water almost to the top. Place in the freezer. After an hour or so, push down any materials that have risen above the thin layer of ice that has formed. Let freeze for twenty-four hours, then unmold by using warm, not hot, water. Once unmolded, the ice bucket can be kept in the freezer until time for the party. Set it on a towel or metal tray to collect the water as the ice melts. This bucket can be made with appropriate flowers throughout the year. However, the simpler the better since it is most beautiful when light comes through the ice. Ilex berries are used in the ice basket. Jeffrey pine branches, red tulips, paper white narcissus, and genista are used in the arrangement next to the ice bucket.*

page 140: Top, Winter Berry Wreath. *Recipe: Cut clusters of berries and fruits from vines, shrubs, and trees. Strip off all leaves. Gather a mixture of the berry and fruit clusters into small, individual bunches and wire each bunch together. Attach the bunches to a homemade or store-bought wire wreath form, packing them together tightly and wiring each securely to the form. Continue working until the wreath is full. Privet berries in wreath, the fruit of fruited ivy, and star eucalyptus berries; mantle covered with a variety of greens, privet berries, and Osage oranges. Bottom,* Holiday Pomander. *Recipe: Use any variety of citrus fruit. Using a sharp needle or skewer, poke holes into the fruits in various designs. Place a whole clove in each hole. To preserve, roll in a mixture of ground cinnamon and orrisroot powder. For added interest, attach star anise or other whole spices using a glue gun.*

page 141: Top, Sugared Fruit. *Recipe: Whip two egg whites until foamy, and paint onto fruit, then dip into superfine sugar. Let dry on a cookie sheet without touching each other. Refrigerate overnight. Lady apples, kumquats, Seckel pears, cherries, key limes, pineapple guava, and tangerines. Bottom,* Ornamental Kale Arrangement: *Ornamental kale, hellebore, ground ivy, and Osage oranges*

pages 142–143: Birdhouse Collection: *A variety of greens, pinecones, Lady apples, and Braeburn apples*

page 144: Red Winter Bouquet: *Pomegranates on branch, Brazilian pink pepper berries, euphorbia, nandina, pink panther, abelia, and Color Magic garden rose*

page 145: Left, Brazilian pink pepper berries with angel face. Top right, Rose and Fresh Currant Bouquet: *Mon Cherie, Othello, and William Shakespeare garden roses, fresh currants, nandina, penstemon. Plums, cherries, figs, pears, grapes, apple, and pomegranate on the table below. Bottom right, Pomegranates on the branch, Brazilian pink pepper berries, nandina, pink panther, abelia, and Color Magic garden rose*

page 146: Left, Pernettya branches on mantle. Top right, Clematis seed clusters on vine and dried thistle flowers. Bottom right, Ice on shrub

page 147: Gilded Acorn. *Recipe: To gild any hard-surfaced material, apply a thin coat of sizing with a brush and let sit until the surface becomes tacky to the touch. Apply gold, silver, or bronze leaf with a burnishing tool, then brush off the loose pieces. This technique can be used on squash, pumpkins, pomegranates, leaves, and eggs, as well as on acorns.*

page 148: Left, Green Walnut Liqueur. *Recipe: Collect three pounds of green walnuts in late May or June and cover them with two quarts of vodka in a large jar. Add one clove and a cinnamon stick. Let stand in a cool, dark place for two to three months. After this time heat four cups of sugar and one-and-a-half cups of red wine to boiling and continue to boil over medium heat until the mixture reduces by half. Let cool. Drain the liquid from the walnuts, discard the walnuts, and combine the liquid well with the wine syrup. Pour through cheesecloth into individual bottles and cork. Let stand for two weeks before serving over custard or ice cream, or as an after-dinner treat. Top right, Pomegranates and chestnuts. Bottom right,* Holiday Greens Arrangement: *Greens with cones, lilac, anemones, paper white narcissus, Star of Bethlehem, and pernettya*

page 149: Winter Evening Mantle: *Dendrobium orchid, Osage oranges, paper white narcissus, and camellia*

page 151: Oak Angel: *Tiny oak galls and leaves with lichen woven into a halo*

pages 158–159: Peony

page 160: Hyacinth bulbs beginning to sprout

Bibliography

The Beacon Book of Quotations by Women, *compiled by Rosalie Maggio, Boston, Beacon Press, 1992.*

Flint, Martha Bockée, A Garden of Simples, *London, Scribner and Sons, 1900.*

Harrison, Michael and Christopher Stuart-Clark, editors, A Year Full of Poems, *London, Oxford University Press, 1991.*

A Gardener's Bouquet of Quotations, *compiled and edited by Maria Polushkin Robbins, New York, Dutton, 1993.*

The following quotations are taken from the aforementioned book: Henry David Thoreau p. 16, Hal Borland p. 20, Mary Webb pp. 26-27, Henry Wadsworth Longfellow p. 41, Vita Sackville-West p. 54, Georgia O'Keefe p. 66, Ruth Stout p. 101, Elizabeth Lawrence p. 105, Shirley Ann Grau p. 118, Andrew Wyeth p. 133, Chinese proverb p. 95

Stewart, Harold, A Net of Fireflies; Japanese Haiku and Haiku Painting, *Boston, Charles E. Tuttle, 1993.*

Strong, Ronald, A Celebration of Gardens, *Portland, Oregon, Sagapress/Timber Press, 1991.*

Wolfenden, Joan, The Glory of the Garden, *Isle of Wight, Great Britain, Cross Print, 1982.*

Zolotow, Charlotte, River Winding, *New York, Harper and Row, 1970.*

Acknowledgements

Our heartfelt thanks to all those whose generosity, talents, and enthusiasm made this book possible. We especially want to thank Jenny Barry, our talented designer and publisher, who believed in us and provided us with the opportunity to work for Collins Publishers San Francisco. We much appreciate her extraordinary effort and involvement in producing a beautiful book that makes us all proud. And to Ethel Brennan, our writer, who was able to put what we were feeling into beautiful prose. She unselfishly provided us with her time and talent, and was always there when we needed her. Lauren Allard added whimsy and romance with her elegant illustrations and calligraphy. We also want to thank her for her willingness to give herself completely to this project whenever we called. And to our copyeditor, Lessley Berry, thank you for your help when we most needed it.

To all those people who assisted us in producing this book, we want to say thank you. To Terry Greene, our photography and styling assistant. To Cachet Bean, who helped organize the slides and generally made working easier for us all. And to Kirstie Laird, Laura Lorenz, Nicole High, Delmy Rivera, and Michele Miller, for their contributions. To Kristen Wurz, Jennifer Grace and Maura Carey Damacion at Collins Publishers, who so generously worked with us and our materials.

To all those friends who opened their homes and gardens to us, we are indebted. These special locations gave the book depth, interest, and a sense of place. We especially want to thank Helie Robertson and Joe Wahnsiedler for letting us photograph their lovely garden over and over again, capturing each season, and enjoying the changes as they appeared. And to Jan Dutton and her family, and Barbara, Spencer, and Lindsey Hoopes for letting us invade their homes at a moment's notice, and for being so generous with their prized possessions. We are equally appreciative of Kathryn Kenna, Lauren and Paul Allard, Sally and Don Schmitt of the French Laundry Restaurant, Mr. and Mrs. Thomas Vella, Gerald Reis, Stephanie LeGras of 20 Ross Commons, Mr. and Mrs. William Birdsey, Lee and Kathy Epstein, Mary Novak of Spottswoode Winery, Paul Harbertz, John Norcross of the University of California Blake Gardens, and to Ellen Calvert who passed away during the production of this book.

We want to say thank you to all those people and shops who shared props and containers with us. Lauren Allard and Alice Erb of Tail of the Yak, Berkeley, were always willing to loan us unique and special pieces from their personal and store collections. To John Nyquist and Charles Gautreaux from Vanderbilt and Co., St. Helena; Bonnie Grossman from the Ames Gallery, Berkeley; Maria Vella of Bomarso, San Francisco; Mike Kothuis of Van Hollandt Artistique, San Francisco; Ken Poisson of Le Poisson Antiques, San Francisco; Sue Fisher King, San Francisco; and Devorah Nussenbaum, we want to express our gratitude.

Many thanks to the following people and growers who went to special efforts to share, send, and give us the natural materials that make an incredible difference in many of the compositions and photos in this book: Ray Giacopazzi of Hillcrest Gardens; Pam and Ron Kaiser of Westside Gardens; Sandy Morril and Kathleen McKeller of Smith and Hawken Nursery, Berkeley; Karen McBride and Leslie Hyche

of Tahoe Tree Company; Jerry Bolduan of Green Valley Growers; Roy Borodkin, Noble Hamilton, Tom Kowalczyk, Rick Dixon, Abbie Zak of Brannon Street Florists; Rosas de Jardin; Vicki Prosek; Bill Fujimoto of Monterey Market; Juna Carle and Robert Ruggeri of Silver Terrace Nurseries; Kozlowski's Berry Farms; Betty Jane Roth, Lida Bissell, LeRoy McKinney, Jeff Dearden, Mary Helen and Jim Bennett, Jerry Maddrill, Laura Lorenz, Clare Webber, Frank Aguis, Emeline Martin, and Mary Hamaji.

And to our very special friends who gave us moral support, advice and encouragement throughout the year, thanks to Cab and Gary Rogers, Jackie Jones, Susan Hastings and Hans Nehme, Pamela and Hally Swan, Carrie Wright, Mary Fitch, Brad Bunnin, Josh Piagentini, Kay Caughren, Claire Niemiste, Carla, David and J.D. Nasaw, and to Georgeanne Brennan, our special angel in the wings. And finally, thank you for the love and support from our partners and families. To Ed Haverty and Michael, Eric and Peter Schwab, thank you for your endless patience and understanding, and especially to Eric, for your photo assistance.

Spring is the next attraction.
How difficult it is to be patient, but
it will come and burst forth once again
into the glory of the garden and
the cycle of the year...

Joan Wolfenden